Greetings
and
Phrases

BY KATHY THORNBOROUGH • ILLUSTRATIONS BY KATHLEEN PETELINSEK

A SPECIAL THANKS TO OUR ADVISERS:
As a member of a deaf family that spans four generations, Kim Bianco Majeri lives, works, and plays amongst the deaf community.

Carmine L. Vozzolo is an educator of children who are deaf and hard of hearing, as well as their families.

The Child's World®

PUBLISHED by The Child's World®
1980 Lookout Drive • Mankato, MN 56003-1705
800-599-READ • www.childsworld.com

ACKNOWLEDGMENTS
The Child's World®: Mary Berendes, Publishing Director
The Design Lab: Design
Jody Jensen Shaffer: Editing

PHOTO CREDITS
© Asier Romero/Shutterstock.com: 7, 22; Boris Ryaposov/
Shutterstock.com: 17; bowdenimages/iStock.com: 21; Dean
Mitchell/iStock.com: 12; deyangeorgiev/iStock.com: 23; franci88.
Shutterstock.com: 6; fotografstockholm/iStock.com: back cover,
14; huronphoto/iStock.com: back cover, 10; jlmatt/iStock.com: 5;
MarkgrafAve /iStock.com: 11; michaeljung/Shutterstock.com: 4;
PathDoc/Shutterstock.com: 8, 16, 20; Patrick Foto/Shutterstock.
com: cover, 1, 3; pzAxe/iStock.com: 18; Richard M Lee/
Shutterstock.com: 13; shipfactory/Shutterstock.com: 19 ;Valeriy
Lebedev/Shutterstock.com: 9; Yuangkratoke Nakhorn/Shutterstock.
com: 15

ISBN 9781626873209
LCCN 2014934487

PRINTED in the United States of America
Mankato, MN
July, 2014
PA02216

NOTE TO PARENTS AND EDUCATORS:

The understanding of any language begins with the acquisition of vocabulary, whether the language is spoken or manual. The books in the Talking Hands series provide readers, both young and old, with a first introduction to basic American Sign Language signs. Combining close photocues and simple, but detailed, line illustrations, children and adults alike can begin the process of learning American Sign Language. Let these books be an introduction to the world of American Sign Language. Most languages have regional dialects and multiple ways of expressing the same thought. This is also true for sign language. We have attempted to use the most common version of the signs for the words in this series. As with any language, the best way to learn is to be taught in person by a frequent user. It is our hope that this series will pique your interest in sign language.

Hello.

"Hello" in Spanish is "Hola."

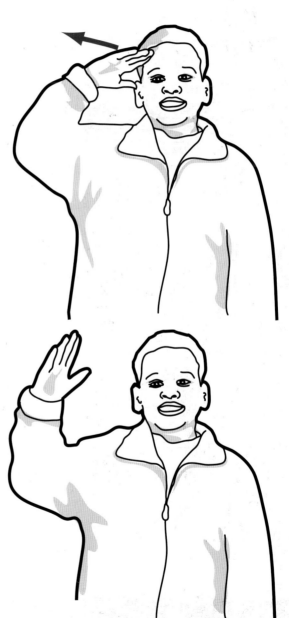

3

Goodbye.

"Goodbye" in French is "Au revoir!"

4

What's your name?

Names sometimes have meanings. The meaning can change with different languages.

Face your flat right hand out. Then make the "H" shape with both hands and tap your fingers together. Face your hands up and move them in and out at the same time.

5

My name is…

Hello
my name is

Name tags help
introduce people.

Pat your chest with your flat right hand. Then make
the "H" shape with both hands and tap them together.

Nice to meet you.

Start with your flat left hand facing up. Keep it still while your flat right hand slides across and off. Then make the "1" sign with both hands. Touch your hands together. Then point at the person you're meeting.

How are you?

Bend your fingers (both hands) toward your chest.
Then rotate your hands so your fingers point up.
Now point your right index finger
at the person you're talking to.

"How are you?" is a nice way to greet someone.

I'm fine.

Saying "I'm OK"
is another way to
say "I'm fine."

Tap your chest with your right index finger.
Then open your right hand and tap
your chest twice with your right thumb.

9

Please.

Put your flat right hand
on your chest. Move it
in a circular motion.

"Please" in German
is "Bitte."

Thank you.

"Thank you" in Japanese is "Arigatoo."

Put your flat right hand on your chin.
Then move it down and away.

You're welcome.

"You're welcome" in Spanish is "De nada."

Flatten your right hand and
move it toward your stomach.

"Excuse me" in French is "Excusez-moi."

Excuse me.

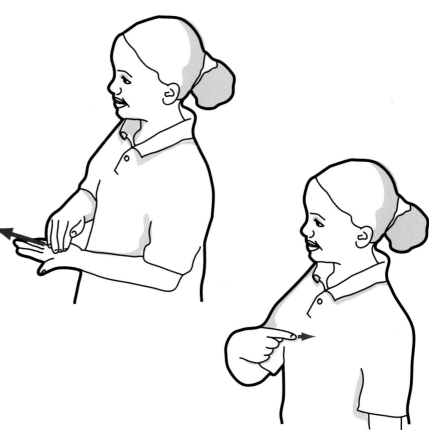

Bend the fingers on your right hand.
Slide them off your flattened left hand.
Then tap your right index finger
on your chest.

Yes.

Make the "S" sign with your right hand.
Move your wrist downward a few times
while nodding your head "yes."

"Yes" in German
is "Ja."

14

No.

Touch the middle and index fingers of your right hand to your thumb while shaking your head "no."

I'm sorry.

Make the "A" sign with your right hand. Then make a circular movement on your chest.

"I'm sorry" in Spanish is "Lo siento."

What time is it?

If you wear a watch, just pointing to it will make this sign.

Make the "X" sign with your right hand.
Tap the back of your left wrist twice.
Then open both hands and move them
in and out at the same time.

17

I like you.

Tap your chest with your right index finger.
Then touch your thumb and middle finger to your chest.
Pull away and close your thumb and middle finger together.
Now point to the person you are talking to.

Help!

"Help me" in French is "Aidez-moi."

Make a fist with your right hand,
keeping your thumb up.
Put your flat left hand
underneath and push up.

Come with me.

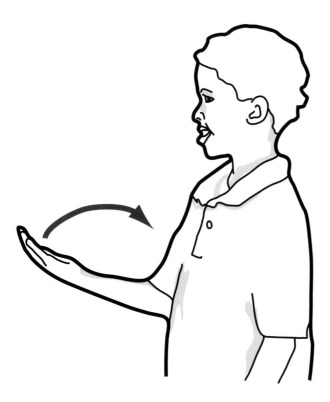

Move your right arm toward your body,
bending your wrist as you go.

Motioning with your
finger is another way
to make this sign.

20

Good morning.

"Good morning" in Japanese is "Ohayoo."

Flatten both of your hands and face them toward you.
Touch your right hand to your chin, then move it downward
into your left hand. Now place your left hand inside your
right elbow. Pull your right hand toward your face.

Good afternoon.

Both of your hands are flat.
Touch your right hand to your chin and move it downward.
Then touch your right elbow with your left index finger.

"Good afternoon" in Spanish is "Buenas tardes."

Good night.

"Good night" in German is "Gute Nacht."

Both of your hands are flat.
Touch your right hand to your chin and move it downward.
Curl your right wrist over your left hand.

A SPECIAL THANK YOU!

A special thank you to our models from the Program for Children Who are Deaf and Hard of Hearing at the Alexander Graham Bell Elementary School in Chicago, Illinois.

Alina's favorite things to do are art, soccer, and swimming. DJ is her brother!

Dareous likes football. His favorite team is the Detroit Lions. He also likes to play video games.

DJ loves playing the harmonica and video games. Alina is his sister!

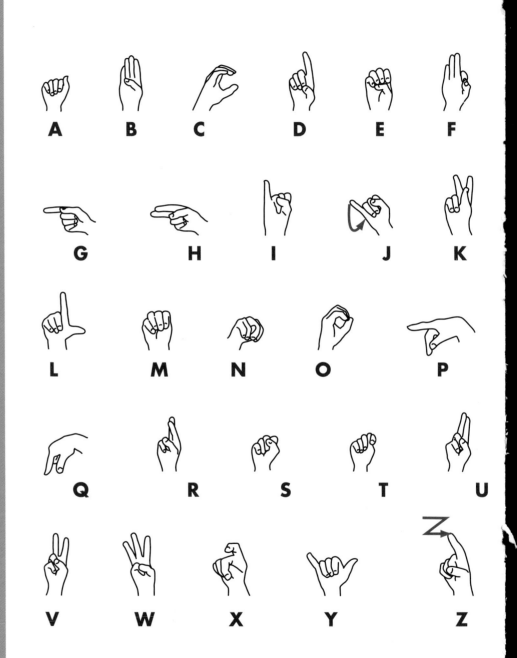